Time's Body

HAGIOS
PRESS

Time's Body

Kathleen Wall

Library and Archives Canada Cataloguing in Publication

Wall, Kathleen, 1950-
    Time's body / Kathleen Wall.

Poems.
ISBN 0-9735567-4-9

    I. Title.

PS8595.A5645T54 2005   C811'.54   C2005-902290-6

Printed and bound in Canada.

HAGIOS PRESS
Box 33024 Cathedral PO
Regina SK S4T 7X2

ACKNOWLEDGEMENTS

I would like to thank the Saskatchewan Writers Guild for their support in the form of a major award for the manuscript that forms the kernel of *Time's Body*. I would also like to thank my "editorial family," Barbara Powell, Kenneth Probert, and Jeanne Shami, for their help with the manuscript.

I am gratfeul to my parents, Doris and Lawrence Wall, for teaching me the delights of craftsmanship, whether with needle, hammer, or words.

My daughter, Veronica, has been the inspiration for many of these poems. "Gratitude" falls far short of what I feel about the richness she brings to my life.

"Ariadne" was first published in the *Antigonish Review*, and "Aphony" in *Canadian Literature*.

The publishers gratefully acknowledge the assistance of the Saskatchewan Arts Board and the Canada Council for the Arts in the production of this book.

Edited by Hilary Clark.

Cover and book design by Donald Ward.

Cover photo: "Autumn Aspens" by Dana White.

Author photo by Don Hall.

Set in Goudy Oldstyle.

CONTENTS

The Painter Sings

Schooling a Daughter

The On-Line Blind Date Poems

Portraits and Elegies

Time's Body

For Jamie Morrison and Barbara Powell

The Painter Sings

PLAYING CHOPIN NEAR AN OPEN WINDOW

On a midsummer night the notes
suspend singly in heavy air
then tumble in damp clusters
clinging to edges human and inhuman
around eyes along temples
shadow the serrated borders of trees
In the garden   spray
complicates the damp evening
catches the unfading strain
until it piles in confusion
among delphinium and nicotiana

The riotous tangent of a nocturne
sings of flesh
and the garden's damp misrule

By late August
the dark nocturnes sing
to earlier evenings
Air dry as yellow leaves
no longer clusters notes
Brushing only hair and cloth
they wind freely through the garden
damp flesh and flowers forgotten
Attenuated phrases lose
their way among the trees
are stretched
to fragile webs of unmarked time.

FIRST FRENCH SUITE: SARABANDE

A Bach Sarabande
seduces a wren
considering
the white birdhouse that hangs
from the ash tree in my back garden.

He is busily out of time,
out of measure, constructing
several twiggy nests
to lure himself a couple of wives
impressed with his real estate holdings —
while the metronome holds me
to a stately virginal pace
drawing details and accidentals into taut lines
battered by longing
but untroubled by disorder.

Still, we dance our song — surprising partners,
this polygamous bird and I.
He sings always with this Sarabande
as if he recognizes in its formal web
some knowledge of himself,
and teaches me the ease of trill
that meanders, leafy,
through baroque brocade.

Bach would approve our disparate duet:
bird all ordered for passion
to fill his round houses
with feather and egg;
and I all passion for this order,
for the marking and making of perfect time.

SECOND FRENCH SUITE: GAVOTTE

This sunset dignifies
the silly geese:
their silhouettes could carve cloud.
Turn the car radio up loud enough,
they are the directed lines of Bach
winging notes toward resolution —
except for the thrum of wings
that twang like rubber bands.

So many strands of flight on the evening edge:
I imagine them ensnaring embers of cloud,
pulling them over the mesh of trees.

I am so distant from their raucous joys
that when they sweep fire overhead
in wind- and bird-blown cloud
cinders and ashes will
fall
into my outstretched
hand.

PRACTICING MOZART'S PIANO SONATA IN A

Always, when I come to the minor variation
a door opens somewhere.

Behind gilded rococo moldings,
through doors barely ajar
I hear whispers
of slippers and silk.

Or a weathered door in a brick wall
frames the mazed walkways of Venice
for an evening stroll,
                    mapless,
                              at dusk;
frames also the quiet anxiety
of counterfeit memories,
and the impossibility of return.
The sound of closing doors echoes
down the stony walk
and leaps the canal.

Most often, though,
a door of stone or roughly painted wood
opens on measured gardens —
vast green rooms of hedged and landscaped time
both labyrinthine and rational.
Corners wind like cochlea, open
on an avenue of limes.
Vistas curve away toward infinity.
The seasons — not mere hours — differ here.
One turns on a cadence
from spare and wintry elegance
to the weight of summer storms.

APHONY

I confess I love
the ambiguity of distance
that transforms
a falling yellow leaf
to fluttered moth —
or moth to leaf.
Does it matter what I name
a vision so apposite,
since moth is transformation
of leaf to wings?

Or the confusion of cornfields
that arrange themselves for an instant
into rows
then disperse to green and flowing chaos.
What word is there for fixed and planted order
that dissolves from any other vantage?

If I knew the names for flight,
for small brown tufts transformed
to quick and silver dips and arcs,
perhaps I could name
lark sparrow
or pine siskin
on wing.
But I have no words
for the calligraphic air they transcribe,
or the way the evening
shifts
beneath a jubilant ideogram of wing.

THE SILENCE OF SPEAKING HANDS

The dumb man's ferret
nuzzles the Irish setter,
glides around the knapsack, then
around its owner's legs.

With flow and whorl of hands he tells the girl
who holds her dog's leash nervously
about his small feral friend.
He touches rounded ears and muzzle,
mimics the animal's impish grace.

The green light in the park
is silent.
Shadows and tendrils of light
deepen the distance between the trees,
their trunks like columns
of a fifteenth century cloister.
We who watch are held
in the antique silence
of proportioned stone and bole and grass
while the speaking hands laugh.

LANDSCAPES WITH ABSENT FIGURE

for Brenda Riches

If I turn very quickly
I can just catch her moving
outside the frame.
Sometimes I glimpse the straight back,
the striding swing of an arm,
the turn of a dancing foot.
Or her hair is spread
over a nearly-defeated back that dissolves
into bruises of color
like a Seurat when you stand too close.

My mind sets her firmly in landscapes —
ours not an interior kind of friendship,
I too empirical for the hopeful furniture
she found comfortable.
I glimpse her on a hill where
in late December's glow and frost
she scatters her dog's ashes in celebration
of his return to place.
She appears in the simple, open fragrance
of wild roses
weeping for her daughter,
her shoulders sharp
against the serrated net of leaves.

What I want is to turn suddenly
without stealth or hope
and find her there, in a landscape whose rightness
embraces her absent form;
a place which folds and shifts like sand dunes,
always familiar, always unknown,
until, like breath shadowed by aspens,
I know her comfort everywhere.

ABOUT SURFACES

How sheer and shiny they seem:
the lake at violet dusk stretched tightly
over the rocks,
the sky beaten to the thinness
of fleeting molecules.

Or my skin — how light from lake and sky
barely grazes its flayed surface
so I crave release from this papery husk —
yet fear that nothing will ever
skim
        or jostle
                or crowd
my nerves again.

And so I need things workmanlike,
pedestrian:
a thermos flask, a pair of gloves, a garden rake.
Or dishes to wash, a coat to mend —
some domestic, focused task.
Something to practice.

STILLED LIFE

an early snowfall

we are frozen in a crystal
of dislocated time

Russian olive
willow
have not shed their leaves

the ash trees glow —
bosc pears against damask

time and air so stilled
that above the pewter lake
cries of birds
shaped like flight
hang soundless in downy throats

NINE MEDITATIONS ON TRANSPARENCY

for Michael

Throughout my whole life, during every minute
of it, the world has gradually been lighting up
and blazing before my eyes until it has come to
surround me, entirely lit up from within.
                                        – Teilhard de Chardin

I
With watercolours, there is no clarity
that is not absence.
But the oil painter
layers the thick, viscous red
to compose
the strawberry's transparent skin.

II
A single monastic toothbrush
propped
in a hotel glass.
White washcloths,
towels smelling of bleach.
The tiny, white-tiled room becomes
dark, opaque, and endless
as de Chirico's streets
arched by threatening shadows.
In the mirror, do you see
something crystalline?
Your skin, without its partners
or its history?

III
The old grow transparent.
First, the bones.
Then, so we may see the clarity
of pure fury or love
the skin across the webbed and stony hands
is stretched like organza
across a young girl's breast.

IV
The top of a grey tabby's head
pressed against your shoulder
is not transparent.

Beneath the rumpled fur
is the clearest of motives.

V
Consider the opacity
of maybe.

VI
The skin under my eyes
is pellucid as a watch glass.
My moods are mottled
as a raven's egg.

VII
Is it clear
that time is pulled by trains
across opaque seas of grass,
that the shift and sway of stars
is time blown forever outward?

VIII
Even before the violin is made,
you can see the clarity
of its voice
by holding the wooden pieces
to the light
and seeing the trees beyond.

IX
Halfway between colour and nothing,
just past winter dusk
is a blue so clear
that an icicle dropping from the eaves
would shatter it.

Schooling a Daughter

WHALE SONG

My daughter, needing a school report on mysteries,
tells her classmates of whales:
how they have no vocal chords
but sing a long song that evolves
across seasons.
How there is, among the tangle of seaweed and coral,
a deep sound channel
where whale song could wrap round the earth
but for the landmasses
that mute this song
rising from nowhere
one can name.

There is no geography for the coastlines,
shingled or sandy,
that stop my songs from wrapping round her:
continents of responsibility and prudent trust
that mute all but the most pedestrian echo
of some song my voice
can not produce.

SNAILS

My daughter's science project —
two snails named black-and-whites
(but creamy brown)
live now in my kitchen.
They remind me, in their mason jar,
of distances
between flesh and shell
breathing and drowning
name and appearance.
The promised algae doesn't green the sunny jar;
they feed — I hope — on goldfish food.

What would their small pain be like?
Inside their perfect whorls, what is hunger?
They nudge plants and glass and one another,
the blind nuzzling of sleepers and infants.
Their antennae-eyes are inscrutable;
nor can I read the groping of their feet.
They worry me.
I turn the jar to harass them to life
and they pull up camp,
rhythmically see-saw through water,
landing stone among stones.

CATERPILLARS

for Liz Read

Midsummer, my daughter sees a narrow dirt road
made into fearful infinity
by the perspective of a caterpillar,
fat and furry, tiger-striped,
and brings him safely home on her palm.
Because he has no language
and because she is kind
she has forested his glass prison with careful variety.
She thinks he will munch leaves to skeletal lace,
his antennae gleefully bobbing as he chews.

But the roots of those antennae tangle
past food to more pressing summons
and a branch my daughter thought was garden
becomes a gallows
as he hangs, head down, twisting,
spinning his shroud-like second womb
where he will dissolve fur and feet,
brain and belly,
to reconvene as airborn kaleidoscope.

But when the first snow
clouds the kitchen windows
no metamorphosis has burst the hanging pod.
Against the snowy light, we can see that his cocoon
is transparent.

He has a different gift,
one you might envy
more than gaudy transformation.
When infinite dirt road resolves
to glassy garden trap,
he translates himself
to nothing.

FORCING NARCISSUS BULBS

A week in the dark
and bulb roots began to finger and scrabble
among the rocks.
Then we let late winter sun transfix
the leaves and spears of blossom,
tugging upwards, stretching green length daily
to an explosion of white fragrance.
Tall in their southern window,
they permeated the house:
I smelled them when I woke in the morning,
or cooked a garlicky curry
or brushed a cat.

After moving for two weeks
along the fragrant paths of narcissi
I found their waxen petals frail,
thinned to transparent webs
as if they'd breathed their pellucid flesh
into our household.

        I pulled them up
wanting to release the nest of stones
clutched to the bulb's under-heart,
        stones we collected on beaches
wild and tame:
quartz fragments
lake-tumbled feldspar lozenges once stranded
in high pools
folded toffee curiosities
limestone balls and basalt eggs that tumbled
with lint and sand in your pocket.

                    Like the baby teeth
I find when I search
for a lost key or spare change,
they sabotage me with memory.
What are these stony memories
entangled in?
What demanded this clutching?
          The hidden, green, unimaginable heart
                    springing
luminously toward the sun
or the earthy insentience of papery bulbs?

CORRESPONDENCE WITH A DAUGHTER STUDYING
THE HISTORY OF ART

Fall

For your monastic room
overlooking roofs of tar and tin
I send you a bit of prairie zen
to mingle with the calculus,
the classical pot shards,
the theories of simulacra and words of Lear.

> September 8:
> Tonight the moon floats
> in a hotblue sky
> like a disciplined cloud.
> Below, the creek's pewter
> silvers and sharpens
> every tuft of golden grass
> every burning leaf
> until a muskrat's ripples
> distort the etching.

> October 2:
> The leaves are fallen, revealing
> the architecture of trees
> the naked flame of golden crabapples
> the bitter red of rose hips and mountain ash.
> In the slanting light of early evening
> the still lives in kitchen windows
> look vulnerable.

I do not write of rifling the photograph album
for a picture of you at fifteen.
In the midday light, the camera has caught you

suspended in a leap
above a pile of leaves.
Grateful for time that does not careen
and hurtle forward
I filch the image from the album's progress
to speak to me of the timelessness of daughters
while I work.

Winter

I am studying the technology
of early Islamic pots,
shaped outwardly, then hollowed.
Hollowed myself, I forbid my moods
to turn transparent, to turn
inside out.

Your world above the roofs
is monochrome with snow and study.
I write you recipes for ninth-century glazes
of turquoise and deep green.
Just before exams,
I send animal jokes of polar bears
who wear fur coats because they'd look ridiculous
in tweed. I write the architectural gossip
about the Getty Museum — how Meier forgot
the public loos.

Everything goes winter brittle:
the handmade paper you use for letters,
your patience with the mental furniture
of your mother's age.
The cord the doctor thought he nipped at birth
twangs and snaps with independence and opinions.

For a thaw I rival Dickens,
send serial postcards from New York galleries
flaunting the hot blue breezes of Provence,
bending poppies,
the unseasonal irises of Van Gogh,
Monet's eternal waterlilies.
On the back I ask questions
about the use of beauty
I hope the philosophers
are teaching you to answer.
Four days before spring
my birthday box arrives
with chocolate Amaretto coffee beans
and the music of Hildegaard.
My address on the paper-covered parcel
is centered in your architectural doodle:
three classically columned arches and a balustrade.
Your address, my address, the postmark
fix us in these separate, timeless rooms.

Spring

In the spring my email resembles the diary
of a hurried Victorian naturalist:
On April first I report five butterflies
and a prairie dog.
On the second, the first robinsong heard above the grackles.
Tulips surging on the sixth.
I send queries about the meaning
of this year's oversized ladybugs.

> Sitting with you in a pile of leaves
> I taught you to count with ladybugs.

You brag about your spring in downtown Montreal —
further along, more colorful,
but lacking the fragrance of newly-dug soil.

Today I walked past the dell
you called your Brandywine river.
I did not tell you that I measured
with a child-sized view
not only the distance from shore to shore
but also the divide between playing hobbit
and reading Kant.

The miracle is this contradictory time of daughters,
the thousand moments flowing
daily in our veins,
the umbilical lines stretched between the prairies and the east
made, impossibly, of nothing but words.

The On-Line Blind Date Poems

DOOMED UNCLE

He comes up the walk
greensuitwhiteshirtgoldtiebrownshoes
looking, for all the world,
like a high school principal.

But I am fifty.

Is the touching calibrated,
metered by propriety?
A guiding hand at my elbow
after dinner and a bottle of wine;
the directing hand at the centre of my back
at intermission;
his hand cupping my shoulder, his face in my hair
during the standing ovation.

He does not know he is doomed by a haircut,
that the thick white hair
cut straight across his nape
reminds me of my Uncle Basil,
who used his white handkerchief to pull my baby teeth
and taught me to like gherkins and black olives.

As we listen to "The Way We Were"
(full orchestra, easy, sidling drums;
the sexiness of romantic strings and night clubs)
another man who sits to my right —
a man older and younger,
less hair, more grey,
dressed in dockers and a fair isle sweater —
slouches toward my shoulder and sleeps.
Accompanying my date's musical critique
I hear the slow dotted rhythm,
the shy intimacy of a sleeper's breath.

ASSUAGE

Today, frugal spring
is beginning to write its prophecies
on the golden parchment of last year's grasses:
a mottled bark-grey, green-golden Mediaeval manuscript
to which a joyous monk is adding serifs of buds
and commas of sedge.

Before the coffeehouse window,
listening to one another's losses,
we study
in our silence
the word *assuage*.

How we illuminate the word differently.
You script a spiky Gothic 𝕬
bristling with past barbs
that trail off into doubt.
While I have been erasing
like a monk with his pumice
the lines on my parchment,
practicing uneven italic circles.

Assuage needs the patience
to read a palimpsest
in numerous hands,
the honesty to admit
that the vanishing point in the tiny spring landscape
curled under the large A
cannot be seen by both of us at once.

THE MID-DATE LECTURE

So (being fifty) we meet in ill-lit coffee houses
trying to defy
the social distances of middle age,
reach across the two feet of propriety
and enter the magnetic field of desire.

Being a woman, my job is to create a vacuum
of attentive silence, virgin territory, a blank
slate where he writes the contradictory tale
of his successful quest (being middle aged)
for a comfortable salary,
the praise (or absence) of superiors, freedom
from the tedium of responsibility.

And I'm willing to go this far: it's part
(being born in the fifties) of the contract.
It's when the mid-date lecture begins,
this excrescence of success,
this paean to his authority, that I balk.
Half an hour on the Gaia principle, Saskatchewan roads
and their relation to the rural economy, post-communist
banking practices in Macedonia, and I have been
transformed
Kafka-like, to a giant ear — or egometer
sensitively calibrated to masculine expertise.

His eyes are fixed just above my shoulder
(near my ear, as a matter of fact)
in a pleased, self-absorbed daze
that is blind and deaf,
that stops my mouth with chunks of soft sweetness —
pastries, chocolates, tortes of his anxiety —
that he keeps behind glass except on blind dates.

What should I do with this glut of silencing sound?
Swallow it down obediently?
Burp politely?
Take the golden butter icing and shape
a blonde helmet?
Start a food fight?

FORBIDDEN TO SAY THE WORD "DESIRE"

After coffee, we'd walked with our elbows
hinting at touch, our blazers
brushing in simple intimacy,
a quiet, clothed rhythm,
a pulse
like the one I'd imagined flexes
the unfurred underside of your wrist
as you reached for the sugar
and your winter clothes retreated
just to your radius.
What do we know of one another,
clad as we are from wrist to neck and ankle,
but lustful fantasies of pulse and sigh?

Today, at dusk, I stood
a oenophile of leaf mold
gulping down earthy air thick
with the red of dogwood bark, gold of willow,
unable to speak.

You have said the most powerful word —
No —
forbidden me to peel back your winter clothes
like willow bark, to smell the ripe sap
beneath your social self,
to break your skin of ice.

MAMMOGRAM

I

The cubicle, pink
with gray trim,
affords small privacy:
I cannot be seen
(though there is no lock)
but any sound —
a derisive laugh, a sigh or sniffle —
would be heard by technicians
who ferry endless films of breasts
between their owners
and one who never sees us
but knows our inner landscapes.

My technician and I have been pretending
that my breasts are slabs of meat
inconveniently sandwiched
between skin and ribs,
balanced either side of my breastbone,
connected to the lymph nodes in my armpit.
See? Even though we tried,
we could not pretend
they were not somehow attached everywhere.

II

If you men cannot conceive of this,
imagine your balls, your prick,
arranged on a metal plate.
We will not squeeze them

as tightly as my breasts.
But still, the arrangement
must be exact.
It may take several minutes
of tiny adjustments
to get your prick just so.
My hands may be cold —
don't jump.
You are going to pretend
that nothing about your body —
least of all this vulnerable bosky frond
with which you do not think
or lift children
or send email —
has anything to do
with tenderness or lust.

III

While I await the verdict,
I imagine going on
a blind date with a mastectomy
which sounds like a title for a bad
self-indulgent expressionist painting —
reds and blacks, bruised purples,
mostly spatters and splashes,
the odd ominous clot of glowing paint.
I'm new at dating: is there still
that terrified, triumphant groping,
that cross between speedometer and compass
that asks how fast we're going
and where our destination is?

And what would mastectomy etiquette be?
"Aren't I life-like"?
"The other one's nicer"?
After childbearing, is a breast
like an appendix or a kidney?

IV

There are no spaces
on the computer dating form
for lapses, disabilities, absence, loss,
no boxes to check
        I cannot remember
                my first kiss
                my ex-husband's blood type
        I routinely forget
                to pick up the drycleaning
                to buy bread and milk
                birthdays
        I cannot
                balance a cheque book
                read a map
                spell *hypocrisy* or *chrysanthemum*
        I have difficulty
                learning to dance
                taking risks
        I have become
                heartless
                breathless
                fearless

Normally,
we do not list prostheses with our faults.

V

Footsteps become omens
with their own significance.
Does the quiet shuffle portend
reluctance,
the determined tread fearless honesty
hardened by practice,
the quick steps my matter-of-fact dismissal?

In this cubicle every sound
seems to mean something.
Even the paper rustling
of the mute grey-haired woman I glimpsed
in hurried retreat down the corridor
sounds embarrassed.
We are fellow inmates
but do not strike up Morse code conversations
on the pink walls.

I am told I can get dressed
They don't even bother with the subtext:
the suspicious spot
has somehow disappeared?
Was never there?
Do they believe,
without the terrifying proof,
I never worried?

Minutes later my fellow inmate
is told the doctor has ordered an ultra-sound.
Which doctor? she wants to know, alarmed.
If it's her own doctor,
this is as it should be,
in the cards,
a precaution.
But if it's that stranger
who never sees us. . . .

The hallway discourages questions
and the frightened technicians offer nothing,
neither comfort nor understanding.
For there is neither.

THE CURVE OF TIME

We're comfortable enough to walk
with our shoulders almost touching,
the poplin and nylon occasionally adding
their whispers to the dialogue.

But I want to touch
something
that in your breathless rush
your fingers (nails chewed to the quick)
have barely grazed.

This is our first date,
but you have a cat that can't be held,
you shred your bread,
your fingers tap your emphases
into the sticky oilcloth
next to a coffee cup you embrace
in your fist.
I cannot imagine your hand
curving
around a clay pot
or your mind around the adagio
of a string quartet.

Is it your bickering with time
that silences me?
Or your antagonism to silence,
useless in a sempiternity
that you cannot score or measure
with words?

THE WOMAN IN GREY

I

Suppose, growing in some icy fissure,
among the cries of sociable penguins, you found
a lone palm tree, its fronds scouring the vast, blue ice
in a green rasp foreign to Antarctica

— or, listening to Gould's *Goldberg* you could feel
the cold cleft between his clarity of touch and line,
and the helpless hum of a life made,
finally, of midnight phone calls
and a concentrated, protective hunch over the keyboard —

you would find nothing less un-at-home in the world
than a woman performing this everyday act
of entering a coffeehouse, ordering a latté,
and turning with feigned calm and assurance
to look for the lone, expectant face.

II

She is wearing a plum suit or a periwinkle dress
and a serene, cheerful smile that is half real:
this is an earnest, deliberate adventure
a leap (Kierkegaardian?) over scorched earth
into a verdant unknown.

As she turns with an easy smile, she glimpses an earlier self:
a woman in grey who, like a perverse Lady of Lost Things,
shimmers with trinkets that imprint the lapels
of a Balmain suit.
The leaper has spotted the blind date
but pauses to examine the grey wraith's baubles:

household objects that twinkle into weapons —
a blue and white pitcher that pours bile,
a silver tray that carries disdain.

III

What will he do with this ghost
which troubles his view of the smiling leaper
in a periwinkle dress? Over the weeks, he talks to the shade
unclasps a trinket
as if he were undoing a button,
doesn't bother to study them
but drops them in his pocket to jingle
among loose change and keys.
They find their way to his bedside table
where he puts his watch,
a pair of candles and two glasses of wine.

When she collects her watch, her rings and earrings,
she idly examines the trifles. Robbed of their glitter
from their time in his pocket amongst real and sterner stuff,
they are tiny enigmas she dimly associates with the play
of his fingers along her spine.

STONE UPON STONE

How is it that when we are not flesh upon flesh —
        quietly studying the wisdom and variety
        of one another's skin,
        poring over lessons of wrinkle and muscle,
        memorizing the geometry
        of curve and slope

        or noisily, listening to another kind of voice
        that has no speech, never translates
        into words but moves
        limbs and lips to silent accord —

How is it that when we are not flesh upon flesh
we are stone upon stone,
mute, stubborn,
deaf?
How effectively your lies wedge
in the small fissures
between us, how tough
the sexless sediment of habit.

And evasions —
like boulders plunging down a rocky canyon,
these silent moments when you keep
yourself to yourself,
while my stomach heaves at the thought
of the impact.
Promises, those little pebbles collected
on nostalgic lakeshores and left in pockets
or in bedside ashtrays
are dropped to mark trails to the future,
then stolen back.

Most troubling are the stories you tell
that make no sense: pictographs
whose troubled spirits tug
at the bedclothes, begging for the narrative
that releases them from their uncertain, unknown roles
in the self-portrait you fashion for me.

Flesh upon flesh
stone upon stone. I will find a landscape
less arid.

THE BLIND DATE'S MEDITATIONS ON LIGHT

The middle-aged blind date
has a repertoire of places—
public, ill-lit, even at midday.
I know the sabotage of fluorescent lights
and check before I leave the house
the under-eye concealer,
I avoid the mad apple of blush
worn by the old and over-eager.

Out of my angst-ridden twenties
and post-partum thirties
I have found myself studying light
as if each day were a fantasia
of stars twirled in a bottle, of Cheshire cat moons
of suns dipped in morning orange juice
or an evening Merlot.

> Fog this morning, light
> like a moon in a glass of milk,
> the trees on the lake's far edge
> a poignant smudge

You bare yourself proudly in open
pretence, but when you bite my tongue
I see a web of shadows not thrown
by a bedside candle, but an intaglio of wire
that obscures me like a woman behind a fretted
convent gate or a dark chador.

                              The early morning light
                              pares the eastern edge
                              off midwinter gloom,
                              picking out the hoarfrost net
                              thrown over the trees
                              until a chiaroscuro tangle rises

You tuck blankets around my feet,
adjust a pillow, fix dinner while you spin
clichés in that dark, erotic voice,
narratives with lengthy settings,
sudden denouements,
no (reported) conflict,
no action on your part, merely a verbal snapshot
of you standing forlorn on a street
you cannot name, building an empty house.

                              For three days, cloud
                              has echoed snow, light so flat
                              the view from every window
                              a claustrophobic piece of
                              parchment,
                              a few calligraphic trees,
                              no distance, nothing
                              I might touch if I dared

You re-learn the art
of unfastening: buttons, hooks, mouths.
And then you open something you cannot close,
to glimpse
the door to a kitchen where a child eats
alone, the drifting world
you have chosen, the physics
of solitude — its pure cosmic distances,

cold stars, its freezing
of disappointment and fear.
You stretch for blue, then blacker blue, trying to find
the end of the universe
to burrow your way out into truest nothing.

> While I chase another kind of
> light,
> the spring quickening
> of golden willow bark
> the whale shine of a child's boot
> in puddles, the riot
> of parrot green
> against a lapis sky

Portraits and Elegies

DAUGHTER AS CHARON

I am your boatman, your ferrywoman.
I have been charged —
gifted — with your passage
across this water that divides
your substance from your shadow.

As you stepped into my skiff
I leaned waterward to balance
and found you weighed nearly nothing.
No matter:
                    we will meander
these grey water meadows
until you do weigh nothing.

And I will tell you the stories of your body
                    (for you will leave it
                    at the bottom of my skiff
                    and step ashore,
                    light with freedom)
how it glided and leapt through time;
how the pleasure of its curves
delighted the air.
With your head in my lap, I will row desultorily
or ship the oars, and drift.
My hands will read over the cocoon
that binds your vulnerable bones
and silently tell of that oldest of all connections
between animal and animal.

When you are ready,
reduced to nothing you want to keep,
I will bring you ashore —
                              and you,
with a penny you saved for the purpose,
will pay your boatman, your ferrywoman.
But since I cannot charge for this shadow
that lies at my feet
I will cast your penny seaward
with wishes, wishes.
And seeing you, a translucent dream,
turn resolutely from me —
                              only then
will I weep.

THE BLAZE OF SELF

Father, I know
your disorienting drive to the airport —
losing your car
as usual
in the parking lot —
has risks and terrors

but flight is the only way I can get back north
where the midwinter light is austere and transparent.

You are backing into the dark.

I tell you stories of your past
to interest you in your self
but they bore you.
Or you are so deaf you hear only
fragments of my fragments?
Who is left?
A conventional man who must carry my suitcase
and pay for our drinks,
who stands next to a wall or counter,
one well-dressed leg, toe pointed,
angled over the other,
nonchalant like Astaire or Bogart
with knee replacements,
hand in his pocket, jingling change,
pretending to whistle.
A man who gives me bear hugs
and whose lips move when he reads.

As my flight touches down, my useless,
eager wish for you
is one last time so grounded
that you know
the intimate friction of all your days —
that you leave your world in a blaze of self
that rivals this arch of northern light.

THE TIME OF TREES AND CLOCKS

for Deborah

We sit in your kitchen
talking of the Norfolk Island Pine
you bought for your daughter's eighteenth birthday —
how it sickened when she did
and whether you should move it to the downstairs room
you've arranged for her return from the hospital.

Your daughter is dying of cancer
and neurosurgeons cannot manage her pain.
She likes her tree,
so maybe it's a more prescient measure
of her life than blood counts and bone scans.

We sit in your kitchen and sing
with the soft voices of children
who don't want anyone to waken
"My Grandfather's Clock"
constructing lines and verses
from remembered rhymes.

Outside the trees shiver
in the dark green prelude to a storm.

Our clear voices are oddly peaceful
as if this childhood ballad of instinctive sympathy,
synchronicity,
makes sudden (childish) sense.

(As if any private death has meaning,
we do not say to one another.)

We can only close windows against the rain
and refuse to speak — even while we study its shape —
of the enormity of your task:
to love your child toward death.

ELEGY

for Judith Defren and Barbara Powell

Standing at your bed
I mourn the coming absence of your body.
Yet death is perhaps no more
than a memory
of friendly touch and conversation
we bear into the morrow
as it disappears.

You mourn your absence from that place
beyond your body
beyond the fleshly limits that daily
wrap you more tightly,
ring round
like swaddling and shroud.

And since I cannot foresee that place
beyond the grip of your hand —
just *now* —
I imagine your ashes
stirred in the garden
blooming your death
into the delicate tenacity of iris.
Interstices of gothic arch along your bones
holding you now so firm to earth
will fly in seeds or feed
the flight of birds.

Ah, this sigh: and then
your eyes flow open.
Light takes root.

INHERITANCE

for my Mother: Florida, February 1985

Strange it was:
          after
funereal weather, heavy February blooms,
the legal phone call: instructions
to gather my half-sister's worldly goods
not wanted
by the auctioneer —

to find one box containing
an empty address book,
Muskegon Chronicle photos of her show dogs
and prize-winning gladiolas,
four formal portraits of her marriage that hid
its history behind her smile,
and seventy-five or eighty years
diminished to a jumble
of snapshots.

Childhood photos of my sister from before
her mother's death reflect sweet beauty,
but for a placid curve
of confident wisdom along her mouth.
                      After
her mother's death the curve shifts
to irony,
her eyes angry, gazing
beyond the photographer, beyond
the room where she poses.

In courtship photos she controls
the irony along her mouth.
Impishness, grateful clinging
have charmed her a husband who stands,
the romantic cliché: supportive, gallant, handsome.
In later years he stoops, bent
by her furious needs.
                              Her face
wrinkles early, each bitter line
betrays her smile. The wisdom
about her mouth has turned to lust
for age and death. Each crease is welcomed.

After her husband's death she disappears
from photographs. Instead there are the dogs
that stray across the picture's edge,
stone townhouses with a plot of petunias,
friends I do not know
posing in plastic lawn chairs,
shading their eyes as if to look
toward the horizon,
not toward a friend with a camera
whose shadow blots the foreground.
Evidence of life spent in strange places
among strangers, recorded, collected
in the ghostly pale colors of her Brownie camera
to map her ghostly world.

In a blurred photo, her husband sits
on the steps with a person I hardly know —
so shaken is my face.
Yet I recognize a dress I made,
a lace collar bought at Kresge's.
I remember my half sister posing us.
Blurred and out of focus,
I am one of the strangers
she made as she wandered among us,
posed dogs,
arranged flowers,
photographed friends,
fixing, arranging,
leaning
into death's stillness.

PRAIRIE ARIADNE

I

Ariadne
is preoccupied with maps, insists
there is some similarity between
the network on her palms
the tracks around her eyes
and the winter mesh of prairie roads.
        All engrave a space
        that becomes a horizon.

She has given up on string, knowing
her spindle weaves forward
to conclude in the frenzied death
of a reluctant monster
prisoner more of his own appetites
than of Daedalus' maze.

Further on, the spinning thins.
A break brings her abandonment,
Theseus' quick boredom.
He can rewind from Naxos
to his singular beginnings.
                No. She prefers
the possibilities invited
by the warp and weft of roads.

II

Followed, the roads flicker black and white,
dramatic, like magpies that settle in the trees
or maps traced on the freedom of wings.

She believes these roads have homely meaning:
they end
not in labyrinthine entrapment
                                    and her brotherly monster
but in yard lights flooding snow.
And beyond that passionless light,
the deeps and smells of early autumn
are poised in the breath and skins of calm animals.

III

Here, it takes little height
to see the curve of earth fall away
beneath
the loping flight of magpies —
a camber so subtle that it looks
infinite today —
though my return
to where I now stand is bound,
this straight road devouring
itself, like the bracelet of stolen, braided hair
circling my wrist.

The bleached, fallow fields
stretch to the simple grey of nostalgia
until hunger, too, tips over the horizon
like the ship of Theseus.
An hour ago, I scattered a flock of blackbirds
that rose, a threatening net, then in unison

tilted toward me the surprise
and shock of red wings.
I do not know what it augurs:
that startling scarlet tearing
the dark net thrown over
descending fields.

The only other labyrinths are bare trees
whose chambers sing with air
whose walls stretch in the wind.

Along this self-devouring road
the bodies of dead animals have silent wounds
like fur-encircled mouths.

IV

Whenever I stand in grey doorways,
my silken cord threaded through blind passages,
hoping it will withstand fraying —
Whenever I stand so —
the string, with all its falseness,
tenses between my fingers.

The hero believes that rewinding the spindle
will mirror unwinding,
believes in the endless patience
of those who await him.

But I could let go.

And when Theseus drew his way back —
my sad half-brother's blood upon his breast
and splashed across his cheek,
claw marks on his shoulder —
more than time had fled.

V

And so, on Naxos, my spindle
in my pocket to guide me always
through my labyrinth
of loss,
I study the mistake,
pull out an arm's length of silk
and think of Theseus' hands
on his sword,
on my shoulders.

And when I wind it up,
seconds later,
nothing is the same, not the strong
hands of Theseus, not my skin.

What ignorance we had of lapsing time,
collapsing space,
that labyrinth
always
embracing our bodies as we loved,
engendering monsters of our own
impearled in the silk I rewound.

REQUIEM

I

Long ago, I gave up on the cosmic:
on understanding the infinity of star-stretched space
or finding the corner where I can be sure
some god resides to take broken souls
      like the twelve-year-old boy who saw
      his mother's lover murdered
      and now feels up girls
      laughs at their fear
                so broken
      kindness
      might exist only
      on a foreign planet, while ours
      wheels wildly away
      from stellar gravity.

Insanely, I sought small certainties:
that summer days lighten at 5 a m,
that black-eyed Susans are perennial.
I made small worlds, was pleased
when the lady bugs thrived
in their pickle jar on the kitchen table.
But when the six-spotted one
stopped eating the aphids
when she tootled around the parsley stems
in crazed eights,
imagination balked;
couldn't give an act meaning,
wondered how she thought

of running loop-the-loops
on air so stilled
it held her weight.
Next morning, I found her upside down
in the jar's grassy bottom,
and my small arrogance met fear.

Like anyone in the face of uncertainty
about lives creaturely and human,
like anyone who sees that glass can be
air or ground,
prison or prism,
I become a fundamentalist.
A dogma of domestic order
is all I have
against the flower of disorder and unknowing.

II

A woman's cells are choked
by other cells gone mad.
                        In the corridor
that smells of powdered shedding skin,
and the fear of souls abandoned by bodies
                            and of closing doors,
I wonder about hourly changes:
cell counts, body counts,   here
                            and elsewhere.
Think: how fast is measurable,
how slow eternal.

"Am I dying?"
I hold her bruised hand to file her nails,
paint them mauve.
I read her poems till she naps.

"They won't tell me if I'm dying."
"We are all dying," is my safe response,
my philosophical lie, this bit of truth.

I would like to send her a basket of fruit
and pack between the lively globes
fireworks; winged things
that skate on thunderstorms;
raspberries wrapped in August;
starlings above an evening river, eating on glide;
a child practicing Bach.

Instead, I take her in a wheelchair,
to tour the hospital grounds.
We will watch
sparrows flicker on mullein stalks,
imagine we smell the river,
take back to her room a bird's nest
grey with seasons of use and absence.

ORIGAMI CRANES

I

On the radio we hear mortar fire, then
the uncomprehending groans
of a journalist taping
his own death.

In Yugoslavia there is war.
Here it is Christmas.
Bluffs have blossomed hoarfrost
as if some gently sentient creature
breathed living fur upon grey webs
or spun crystals for wintry leaves.

How many of those crystals sang or swayed
as dying breath
or coursed along veins that throbbed with panic

and so sing here now along the wind?

II

"But we are not afraid any more
because we have no hope,"
says Kata Juros, her words
translated from Croatian to English
from voice to fuzzy newsprint.

Whatever sounds that wove into her voice
when she made love —
a note like the useless joy of wrens
or aspen whisper
in her lover's ear —
have been flattened by mortars.

III

A woman folds an origami crane
and tells her anxious child,
whose father's skull lies in some killing field,
to wait! stand still!
                    And as she works, she shows him
          how the complex folds are long unfinished.
          How death in the valley folds inward
          to requiem, elegy,
          blooms when folded
          into winter mountains.
          How beak and wings arise from the same source,
          though one speaks of our tie to earth,
          one to transcendence.
She folds and bends.
                    Then
blows until the paper body breathes,
                              takes wing.

VISITING THE BLIND

Your hospital room is filled
with silence. Not quiet:
the hallways chatter and clack
with orderlies and mops;
bland-footed women crash metal meal trays
as they wordlessly bring food for the blind.
Nurses push carts laden with dressings and equipment
for tests with unsayable names
and purposes no one wants to speak of.   No.
It is silence that twists and turns in the air
between these thin, railed beds,
silence more corporeal
than the bleached cotton curtains
that make a flimsy privacy
meaningless to the blind.
You are secluded only
by the disorder of strange rooms
you cannot map.

At the next bed, ardent, white-gowned voices
beg a man to stop his drinking.
Unable to match our silence with deafness,
we hear the threat frosting the edges
of encouragement and cajollery.
When his wife arrives,
apologizes for being late, for the weather,
for the car, for mismanagement of time,
expressionless, defensive silences open
between her carefully flattened words.

I have not told you of driving out to watch
last night's meteor showers, Perseids
tracing blue Haggia Sophia with wakes of light.
There were other gestures
along the unlit road:
the deeply layered rustle of an unseen aspen,
the smell of fresh-cut hay.

Without pity I could have told you of these.
But what meaning have they
apart from that blazoned vault of darkness
so unlike your own?

Time's Body

OPENING TIME

Entering the room on the beat
between phrase and phrase
I hear the words "opening time"
and see — not a pub erupting in sudden liveliness
but a pomegranate's leather skin being peeled away
to reveal the tangy, jewelled seeds,
each with time's unyielding centre.
And opening time further
with the fervour of the middle aged,
I burst some gems with my clumsy thumb
and then the seeds begin to pour out easily,
hitting the scrubbed pine table, becoming
gnomes and hobbits and elves,
two cats washing one another's faces,
an old teddy bear whose head turns aside wisely,
a whole line of tiny students marching around
newspapers, a quilt, topiary horses:
a whole miniature world on a worktable.
And then I open another segment — oh, I am opening time
with a glorious, despairing vengeance:
here's a skinned knee,
the corner of my daughter's lost algebra homework,
a window sill with chipped paint, unplanted bulbs,
an unfulfilled sneaker heading somewhere on its own,
a broken saucer.
A whirl of unraked leaves obscures it all.

How to measure in this chaos,
this jumble of opened time,
the rich texture and delight
that unites the papery skins of unplanted bulbs
and the fur of a well-loved bear
against the detritus of the never done.

TIME TRAVEL

for Deborah and Jamie

I

The tricks one learns, travelling with children.
To play word games or make Möbius loops
while you wait on two-lane roads
for the construction crew to open the single lane to you,
fresh tar and alfalfa arguing in your nose.

At first, it's the single twist that fascinates,
the confusion of inside and outside,
the doubling of what's divided, the play
of surfaces.

The young man's sign changes
from "stop" to "slow," the Möbius strip slithers
down the side of the seat to remind me —
two weeks later, after we have pulled time behind us
across prairies, through gorges, around badlands,
over hills thrust up by amethyst caves —
of time's surfaces and enchainments as I clean out the car:

How I expect time passes only where I am.
Too easily surprised, I resent
how much slips past behind my back:
flirtatious rosebuds become hips,
the sleeping habits of cats tune to another body,
unshovelled snow hardens to domestic glaciers.
My geography is the location of my time
while Time has another surface that loops and slides on
where I'm not looking.

II

Our senses contradict watches and calendars.
In the young light of a spring morning,
the still light of fall, with its patina
of old paintings,
is evoked by a ripe pear from another hemisphere.
The skin's time is stroked by confused currents of evening air
 — cool from lake and trees, gusts of hidden heat —
that turn on the surface of time to release the smell
of bleached cotton bathing suits and sneakers worn
without socks,
the asexual grit of sand in the crotch of a wet swimsuit,
transforming an evening walk
into the whole aura of summer
swimming in stream-fed lakes
and into the airy mood that comes from being hungry
and not caring.

Or the smell of wood smoke on an early summer day
flashes forward to autumn, twists
back to a ten-year-old memory of early fall at the cottage,
every waking moment in the early chill
infused with woodsmoke and with the heedless joy
of not knowing the date
and of eating fresh bread and cheese
and new apples for dinner.
The shorthand of the senses
leaps the memory to retrieve the texture of bread,
the crunch of apples —
a mood one wants to inhabit
coming round again and speaking
of the body's time.

FICTIONS OF TIME

> I outline a princess, an ordinary one, emaciated
> fashion-model torso and infantile face, like
> those I did for *Favourite Fairy Tales*. Earlier,
> they annoyed me, the stories never revealed
> the essential things about them, such as what
> they ate or whether their towers and dungeons
> had bathrooms, it was as though their bodies
> were pure air. It wasn't Peter Pan's ability to fly
> that made him incredible for me, it was the
> lack of an outhouse near his underground
> burrow.
>
>   – Margaret Atwood
>   *Surfacing*

It's not the absence of fictional outhouses I obsess about,
it's the fictional bounty of time, its apparent elasticity,
a day stretching to contain whatever plot dictates.

How fictional heroines never get in the wrong line
at the grocery store
behind someone who's run out of cheques
and whose credit card won't clear;
how little time they spend scouring the bathtub
and cleaning the toilet;
how the laundry, *sans* apprentice, folds itself fragrantly;
how cooking is the time of seasonable pleasure,
not the chopping of onions and mushrooms,
the spilling of flour,
or the washing of oversized pots
and the carrying out of compost in the rain.

Heroines live where time is only the passing of words
wrapped like print from line to line, page to page,
where time is a coherent, grammatical flow,
a language they speak and direct.

But time is a babble, a Babel,
a bubble:
a sunny afternoon is half
the length of a cloudy one;
Saturdays shorter than Mondays,
shrinking inexplicably toward later afternoon.
Try to establish a grammar of duties,
and a Turrette's explosion of nonsense —
a car accident or someone's time-consuming sadness
or an oven that won't work
or construction on the only route between here and there —
makes cacophony of time:
a Swiss ringing of bells and cuckoos in different keys
beeping of Swatch watches
marks time's flight.

WEEDS

What grows in time's cracks,
in those moments when I cannot move
time forward
with doing? Bright, weedy moments,
easily dispersed.

My daughter's fever
suspends me —
aspirin, juice,
fetched and swallowed —
like the downy feather afloat
on a branch outside her window.

The present abandons us
while I heal time and my daughter
with past pleasures. We re-read
old books, tell family stories.
Between her laboured breaths, I pinch
earlier moments between my fingers
like pages shaken loose from ill-bound volumes.
Comedy. Tragedy. That unnamed balance
in between that art is deaf to.

I make brief forays to the kitchen like a furtive
animal along a forest path, make detours to gather
mail and newspaper, gloss over the guilt
packed in my briefcase, bring back tempting
raspberry juice and cookies.

A square of sunlight frames the shadows
of branch and feather
and moves along the blue-green wall
like a mezzotint we don't know where to hang
engraved with fear and deep calm.

I wait for the feather
to take a deep breath,
float downward,
abandon us.

TIME'S BODY

I

Time's body is not a woman's —
all cycles and curves and circles
a large breasted woman
in a round circus tent
juggling a croquet ball, two pingpong balls,
an egg, a planet or two,
dropping nothing but always tired.

Rather, time's body is an ascetic monk's —
the minutes drop straight
from a bony shoulder
draped in the brown wool of clocks —
an itchy prickly covering,
a robe for timed rituals
of lauds and matins.

II

What is time? asked Augustine.
If it exists, where does it come from,
where does it go?
He did not peel apples,
or he would have watched time
                        spiraling
in the fall of peel
would have known that time telescoped into time,
as the apples transubstantiated,
becoming first savory delight,
then the germ of a thought coming to fruition tomorrow.
The peels themselves have a future: the spinster cook

throws her longest peel over her shoulder
predicts the name of her husband,
then takes the peelings and cores to the compost where
they will bloom
in next year's potatoes.

Time's body is an unstilled life,
a woman juggling an egg
and a planet,
peeling an apple.